School Years Record

A Keepsake Record
from Nursery School to
High School Graduation

Written and Illustrated by

Julie Karen

LONGMEADOW
P R E S S

Published by
Longmeadow Press
201 High Ridge Road, Stamford, CT 06904

Cover design by Julie Karen
Interior design by Julie Karen

ISBN: 0-681-41460-X

Printed in Singapore

First Edition

0 9 8 7 6 5 4 3 2 1

Laughing, singing, having fun

Sunny, happy, breezy

Crying, hurting, finding out

That life's not always easy

Winning, losing, starting new

Wanting to quit, now and then

Learning, growing, moving on

Laughing and singing again

Nursery School

First Day Photo

Name of the school _____

How you got there _____

Your teacher's name _____

Friends in your class _____

Things you learned and liked _____

_____

_____

You didn't like _____

_____
year

Summer

What we did _____
_____
_____

Places we went _____
_____
_____

Holidays

Occasion _____
What we did _____
_____

Occasion _____
What we did _____
_____

Occasion _____
What we did _____
_____

Thoughts About You

From Mom _____
_____
_____

From Dad _____
_____
_____

Fifth Birthday

How we celebrated _____

_____

Who came to celebrate _____

_____

_____

Gifts

Who from	*Gift*
_____	_____
_____	_____
_____	_____
_____	_____
_____	_____

photo

10

Kindergarten

Name of school _____

How you got there _____

Your teacher's name _____

What your teacher says about you _____

_____

What you liked to do best _____

_____

Friends _____

_____

Other activities _____

Writing your name   A drawing by you

_____

– – – – – – – – – – – – – – – –

_____

school photo

_____
year

Summer

What we did _____
_____
_____

Places we went _____
_____
_____

Holidays

Occasion _____
What we did _____
_____

Occasion _____
What we did _____
_____

Occasion _____
What we did _____
_____

Thoughts About You

From Mom _____
_____
_____

From Dad _____
_____
_____

Sixth Birthday

How we celebrated _____

Who came to celebrate _____

_____

_____

Gifts

Who from   Gift

_____ | _____
_____ | _____
_____ | _____
_____ | _____
_____ | _____
_____ | _____

photo

First Grade

Name of the school _____

How you got there _____

Your teacher's name _____

What your teacher said about you _____

_____

_____

Friends _____

_____

_____

Favorite subjects _____

_____

Your Report Card

Subject	Grade

Subject	Grade

After school activities _____

_____

Sports you played _____

_____

First Grade

Homework _____

_____

After school chores _____

_____

_____

Sample of your writing   A drawing by you

_____

- -

_____

school photo

year

Summer

What we did _____

_____

_____

Places we went _____

_____

_____

Holidays

Occasion _____
What we did _____

_____

Occasion _____
What we did _____

_____

Occasion _____
What we did _____

_____

Thoughts About You

From Mom _____

_____

From Dad _____

_____

_____

Seventh Birthday

How we celebrated ―――――――――――――――――――――――――

―――――――――――――――――――――――――――――――――――

Who came to celebrate ―――――――――――――――――――――

―――――――――――――――――――――――――――――――――――

―――――――――――――――――――――――――――――――――――

Gifts

Who from	Gift

photo

Second Grade

Name of the school ⟶ _____

How you got there _____

Your teacher's name _____

What your teacher said about you _____

_____

Friends _____

_____

Favorite subjects _____

_____

Your Report Card

Subject	Grade

Subject	Grade

After school activities _____

Sports you played _____

_____

Second Grade

Homework _____

_____

After school chores _____

_____

_____

Sample of your writing   A drawing by you

_____

_ _ _ _ _ _ _ _ _ _ _ _ _

_____

school photo

Summer

What we did _____
_____
_____

Places we went _____
_____
_____

Holidays

Occasion _____
What we did _____
_____

Occasion _____
What we did _____
_____

Occasion _____
What we did _____
_____

Thoughts About You

From Mom _____
_____
_____

From Dad _____
_____
_____

Eighth Birthday

How we celebrated _____

_____

Who came to celebrate _____

_____

_____

Gifts

Who from   *Gift*

_____   _____

_____   _____

_____   _____

_____   _____

_____   _____

_____   _____

_____   _____

photo

Third Grade

Name of the school _____

How you got there _____

Your teacher's name _____

What your teacher said about you _____

_____

_____

Friends _____

_____

_____

Favorite subjects _____

_____

Your Report Card

Subject	Grade		Subject	Grade

After school activities _____

_____

Sports you played _____

_____

Third Grade

Homework _____

_____

After school chores _____

_____

_____

Sample of your writing   A drawing by you

_____

- -

_____

school photo

Summer

What we did _____

_____

_____

Places we went _____

_____

_____

Holidays

Occasion _____
What we did _____

_____

Occasion _____
What we did _____

_____

Occasion _____
What we did _____

_____

Thoughts About You

From Mom _____

_____

_____

From Dad _____

_____

_____

Ninth Birthday

How we celebrated _____
_____

Who came to celebrate _____
_____
_____

Gifts

Who from	Gift

photo

25

Fourth Grade

Name of the school —————————————————————————————

How you got there ——————————————————————————————

Your teacher's name —————————————————————————————

What your teacher said about you ——————————————————————

———

———

Friends ——————————————————————————————————————

———

———

Favorite subjects ————————————————————————————————

———

Your Report Card

Subject	Grade		Subject	Grade

After school activities ——————————————————————————————

———

Sports you played ————————————————————————————————

———

Fourth Grade

Homework _____

_____

After school chores _____

_____

_____

Sample of your writing

_____

_____

_____

school photo

Summer

What we did _____

_____

_____

Places we went _____

_____

_____

Holidays

Occasion _____
What we did _____

_____

Occasion _____
What we did _____

_____

Occasion _____
What we did _____

_____

Thoughts About You

From Mom _____

_____

From Dad _____

_____

Tenth Birthday

How we celebrated _____

_____

Who came to celebrate _____

_____

_____

Gifts

Who from	*Gift*

photo

Fifth Grade

Name of the school _____

How you got there _____

Your teacher's name _____

What your teacher said about you _____

_____

Friends _____

_____

Favorite subjects _____

_____

Your Report Card

Subject	Grade

Subject	Grade

After school activities _____

_____

Sports you played _____

_____

Fifth Grade

Homework _____

_____

After school chores _____

_____

_____

Sample of your writing

_____

_____

_____

school photo

Summer

What we did _____

_____

_____

Places we went _____

_____

_____

Holidays

Occasion _____
What we did _____

_____

Occasion _____
What we did _____

_____

Occasion _____
What we did _____

_____

Thoughts About You

From Mom _____

_____

From Dad _____

_____

_____

Eleventh Birthday

How we celebrated _____

Who came to celebrate _____

_____

_____

Gifts

Who from

Gift

_____

_____

_____

_____

_____

_____

photo

33

Sixth Grade

Name of the school _____

How you got there _____

Your teacher's name _____

What your teacher said about you _____

_____

_____

Friends _____

_____

Favorite subjects _____

_____

Your Report Card

Subject	Grade

Subject	Grade

After school activities _____

_____

Sports you played _____

_____

Sixth Grade

Homework _____

_____

After school chores _____

_____

_____

Sample of your writing _____

_____

_____

school photo

Summer

What we did _____

_____

_____

Places we went _____

_____

_____

Holidays

Occasion _____

What we did _____

_____

Occasion _____

What we did _____

_____

Occasion _____

What we did _____

_____

Thoughts About You

From Mom _____

_____

_____

From Dad _____

_____

_____

Twelfth Birthday

How we celebrated _____

_____

Who came to celebrate _____

_____

_____

Gifts

Who from   _Gift_

_____   _____

_____   _____

_____   _____

_____   _____

_____   _____

_____   _____

photo

Seventh Grade

Name of the school _____

How you got there _____

Your teacher's name _____

What your teacher said about you _____

_____

_____

Friends _____

_____

_____

Favorite subjects _____

_____

Your Report Card

Subject	Grade

Subject	Grade

After school activities _____

_____

Sports you played _____

_____

Seventh Grade

Homework _____

_____

After school chores _____

_____

_____

Sample of your writing _____

_____

_____

_____

school photo

39

_____
year

Summer

What we did _____
_____
_____

Places we went _____
_____
_____

Holidays

Occasion _____
What we did _____
_____

Occasion _____
What we did _____
_____

Occasion _____
What we did _____
_____

Thoughts About You

From Mom _____
_____
_____

From Dad _____
_____
_____

Thirteenth Birthday

How you celebrated _____

_____

Who was there _____

_____

_____

Gifts

Who from	Gift
_____	_____
_____	_____
_____	_____
_____	_____
_____	_____
_____	_____

photo

Eighth Grade

Name of the school ————————————————————————

Friends ————————————————————————————

————————————————————————————————

Favorite subjects ——————————————————————————

————————————————————————————————

School activities ——————————————————————————

————————————————————————————————

————————————————————————————————

Your Report Card

Subject	Teacher	Grade

After school activities —————————————————————

————————————————————————————————

Sports you played ——————————————————————————

————————————————————————————————

42

Eighth Grade

Homework _____

_____

After school chores _____

_____

_____

Allowance _____

Special Events _____

_____

_____

_____

_____

school photo

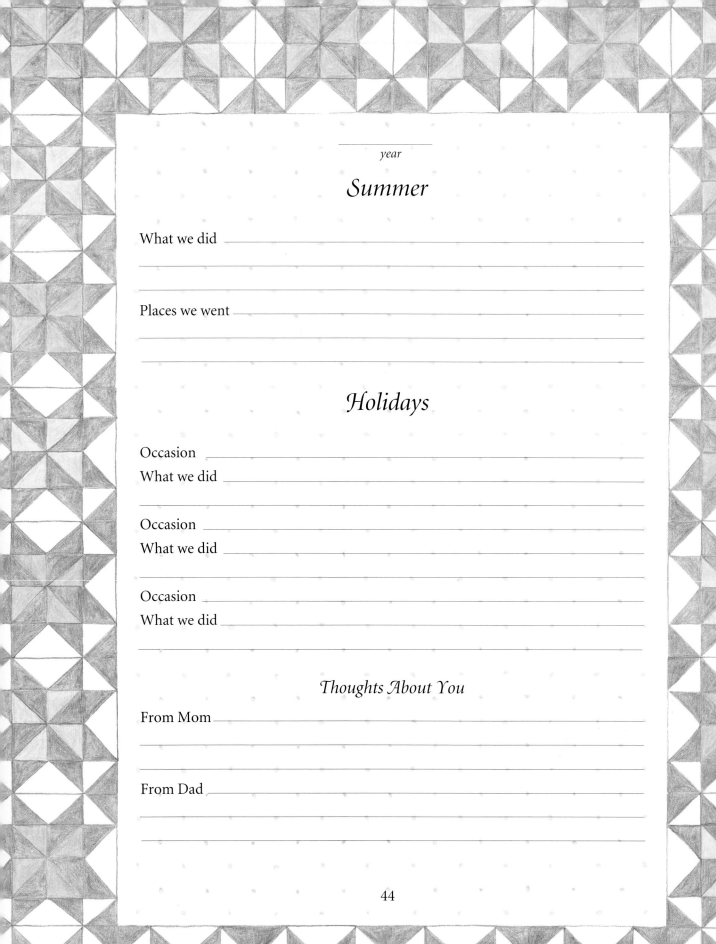

year

Summer

What we did _____

_____

_____

Places we went _____

_____

_____

Holidays

Occasion _____

What we did _____

_____

Occasion _____

What we did _____

_____

Occasion _____

What we did _____

_____

Thoughts About You

From Mom _____

_____

_____

From Dad _____

_____

_____

44

Fourteenth Birthday

How you celebrated _____

_____

Who was there _____

_____

_____

Gifts

Who from   *Gift*

_____   _____

_____   _____

_____   _____

_____   _____

_____   _____

_____   _____

photo

Ninth Grade

Name of the school ⎯⎯⎯⎯⎯⎯⎯⎯⎯⎯⎯⎯⎯⎯⎯⎯⎯⎯⎯⎯

Friends ⎯⎯⎯⎯⎯⎯⎯⎯⎯⎯⎯⎯⎯⎯⎯⎯⎯⎯⎯⎯⎯⎯⎯⎯⎯

⎯⎯⎯⎯⎯⎯⎯⎯⎯⎯⎯⎯⎯⎯⎯⎯⎯⎯⎯⎯⎯⎯⎯⎯⎯⎯⎯⎯⎯

Favorite subjects ⎯⎯⎯⎯⎯⎯⎯⎯⎯⎯⎯⎯⎯⎯⎯⎯⎯⎯⎯⎯

⎯⎯⎯⎯⎯⎯⎯⎯⎯⎯⎯⎯⎯⎯⎯⎯⎯⎯⎯⎯⎯⎯⎯⎯⎯⎯⎯⎯⎯

School activities ⎯⎯⎯⎯⎯⎯⎯⎯⎯⎯⎯⎯⎯⎯⎯⎯⎯⎯⎯⎯

⎯⎯⎯⎯⎯⎯⎯⎯⎯⎯⎯⎯⎯⎯⎯⎯⎯⎯⎯⎯⎯⎯⎯⎯⎯⎯⎯⎯⎯

Your Report Card

Subject	Teacher	Grade

After school activities ⎯⎯⎯⎯⎯⎯⎯⎯⎯⎯⎯⎯⎯⎯⎯⎯

⎯⎯⎯⎯⎯⎯⎯⎯⎯⎯⎯⎯⎯⎯⎯⎯⎯⎯⎯⎯⎯⎯⎯⎯⎯⎯⎯⎯⎯

Sports you played ⎯⎯⎯⎯⎯⎯⎯⎯⎯⎯⎯⎯⎯⎯⎯⎯⎯⎯⎯

⎯⎯⎯⎯⎯⎯⎯⎯⎯⎯⎯⎯⎯⎯⎯⎯⎯⎯⎯⎯⎯⎯⎯⎯⎯⎯⎯⎯⎯

Ninth Grade

Homework _____

_____

After school chores _____

_____

_____

Allowance _____

Special Events _____

_____

_____

_____

_____

school photo

Summer

What we did _____

_____

_____

Places we went _____

_____

_____

Holidays

Occasion _____

What we did _____

_____

Occasion _____

What we did _____

_____

Occasion _____

What we did _____

_____

Thoughts About You

From Mom _____

_____

_____

From Dad _____

_____

_____

Fifteenth Birthday

How you celebrated _____

_____

Who was there _____

_____

_____

Gifts

Who from	*Gift*
_____	_____
_____	_____
_____	_____
_____	_____
_____	_____
_____	_____

photo

Tenth Grade

Name of the school _____

Friends _____

_____

Favorite subjects _____

_____

School activities _____

_____

_____

Your Report Card

Subject	Teacher	Grade

After school activities _____

_____

Sports you played _____

_____

Tenth Grade

Homework _____

_____

After school chores _____

_____

_____

Allowance _____

Special Events _____

_____

_____

_____

school photo

51

Summer

What we did _____

_____

_____

Places we went _____

_____

_____

Holidays

Occasion _____

What we did _____

_____

Occasion _____

What we did _____

_____

Occasion _____

What we did _____

_____

Thoughts About You

From Mom _____

_____

_____

From Dad _____

_____

_____

Sixteenth Birthday

How you celebrated ———————————————————————

Who was there ——————————————————————————

————————————————————————————————————

Driving ——————————————————————————————

Gifts

Who from	*Gift*
———————————	———————————
———————————	———————————
———————————	———————————
———————————	———————————
———————————	———————————
———————————	———————————

photo

Eleventh Grade

Name of the school _____

Friends _____
_____

Favorite subjects _____
_____

School activities _____
_____
_____

Your Report Card

Subject	Teacher	Grade

After school activities _____
_____

Sports you played _____
_____

Eleventh Grade

Homework _____

After school chores _____

_____

Allowance _____

Special Events _____

_____

Junior Prom _____

_____

_____

_____

school photo

_____ *year*

Summer

What we did _____

_____

_____

Places we went _____

_____

_____

Holidays

Occasion _____

What we did _____

_____

Occasion _____

What we did _____

_____

Occasion _____

What we did _____

_____

Thoughts About You

From Mom _____

_____

_____

From Dad _____

_____

_____

Seventeenth Birthday

How you celebrated _____

Who was there _____

_____

_____

Gifts

Who from

Gift

_____ _____

_____ _____

_____ _____

_____ _____

_____ _____

_____ _____

photo

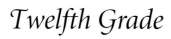

Twelfth Grade

Name of the school —————————————————————

Friends ——————————————————————————

—————————————————————————————————

Favorite subjects ————————————————————————

—————————————————————————————————

School activities —————————————————————————

—————————————————————————————————

—————————————————————————————————

Your Report Card

Subject	Teacher	Grade

After school activities ———————————————————

—————————————————————————————————

Sports you played —————————————————————

—————————————————————————————————

CONGRATULATIONS

Twelfth Grade

Homework _____

_____

After school chores _____

_____

_____

Allowance _____

Special Events _____

_____

Senior Prom _____

_____

Graduation _____

_____

_____

prom photo   *graduation photo*

CONGRATULATIONS

year

Summer

What we did _____

_____

_____

Places we went _____

_____

_____

Holidays

Occasion _____

What we did _____

_____

Occasion _____

What we did _____

_____

Occasion _____

What we did _____

_____

Your Future Plans

_____

_____

_____

_____

_____

_____

CONGRATULATIONS

Eighteenth Birthday

How you celebrated _____

_____

Who was there _____

_____

_____

Gifts

Who from   *Gift*

_____   _____

_____   _____

_____   _____

_____   _____

_____   _____

_____   _____

_____   _____

photo

CONGRATULATIONS